P9-CCE-213

WITHDRAWN

ROCKFORD PUBLIC LIBRARY

3 1112 017814324

J 940 LIN
Lindeen, Mary
Europe

071510

ROCKFORD PUBLIC LIBRARY

Rockford, Illinois

www.rockfordpubliclibrary.org

815-965-9511

EARTH'S CONTINENTS

Europe

by Mary Lindeen

ROCKFORD PUBLIC LIBRARY

Europe is the second-smallest **continent** in the world. Only Australia is smaller.

Arctic Ocean

EUROPE

NORTH AMERICA

Atlantic Ocean

ASIA

AFRICA

Pacific Ocean

Pacific Ocean

SOUTH AMERICA

Indian Ocean

Atlantic Ocean

AUSTRALIA

N
W — E
S

ANTARCTICA

Europe is one of seven continents on Earth.

The Atlantic Ocean is west of Europe. Asia is to the east. Because it has water on three sides, Europe has a lot of **coastline**.

This coastline in England, a European **country**, is rocky.

Many cities in Europe were built near the water. It was easy for ships to sail in and out of these cities.

Ships docked along the coastline in Greece, a European country.

Today there are many big cities in Europe. These cities are very old. They have both old buildings and new buildings.

The European city of London, England, has both old and new buildings.

There are mountains and forests in Europe. Many visitors who go to Europe enjoy downhill skiing.

Skiing is popular in some areas of Europe.

Much of Europe is flat **grassland**. People have been farming such areas for thousands of years. Crops such as barley, wheat, and oats are common.

These tulips are raised in the rich farmland of Holland.

Some places in Europe are near the **North Pole**. It is very cold in those countries for most of the year.

This reindeer lives in northern Europe.

Other places in Europe are near southern seas such as the Mediterranean Sea. It is very warm there most of the year.

Some areas in southern Italy have warm beaches.

There are many places of **natural** beauty to see in Europe. Lake Ladoga is one popular place to see.

Lake Ladoga is the largest lake in Europe. It is in the country of Russia.

There are also many well-known buildings to see in Europe. What would you like to see if you go to Europe?

Many visitors to Europe see the Eiffel Tower in Paris, France.

Glossary

coastline (KOHST-line): A coastline is the spot where the ocean meets land. Cities were built near the European coastline.

continent (KON-tuh-nent): A continent is one of seven large land areas on Earth. Europe is a continent.

country (KUN-tree): A country is an area of land with its own government. France is one country in Europe.

grassland (GRASS-land): A grassland is a large open area of grass where animals can graze. Farmers use grassland in Europe for farmland.

natural (NACH-ur-ull): Something that is natural is made by nature, not by people. Some natural parts of Europe's landscape are beautiful.

North Pole (NORTH POHL): The North Pole is the most northern place on Earth. The coldest places in Europe are near the North Pole.

To Find Out More

Books

Fowler, Allan. *Europe*. Danbury, CT: Children's Press, 2002.

Kalman, Bobbie, and Rebecca Sjonger. *Explore Europe*. New York: Crabtree Publishing, 2009.

Sayre, April Pulley. *Europe*. Brookfield, CT: Millbrook Press, 2003.

Web Sites

Visit our Web site for links about Europe:
childsworld.com/links

Note to Parents, Teachers, and Librarians: We routinely verify our Web links to make sure they are safe and active sites. So encourage your readers to check them out!

Index

About the Author

Mary Lindeen is an elementary school teacher who turned her love of children and books into a career in publishing. She has written and edited many library books and literacy programs. She also enjoys traveling with her son, Benjamin, whenever and wherever she can.

On the Cover: Skiing is popular in this northern village in Switzerland.

Published by The Child's World®
1980 Lookout Drive • Mankato, MN 56003-1705
800-599-READ • www.childsworld.com

ACKNOWLEDGMENTS
The Child's World®: Mary Berendes, Publishing Director
The Design Lab: Design, page, and map production
Red Line Editorial: Editorial direction

PHOTO CREDITS: iStockphoto, cover, 7; David Hughes/Shutterstock, 5; Thamer Altassan/Shutterstock, 9; nikolpetr/Shutterstock, 11; Jaap Hart/iStockphoto, 13; Andreas Gradin/iStockphoto, 15; Natallia Rasadka/iStockphoto, 17; Tokar Dima/Shutterstock, 19; Justin Williford/Shutterstock, 21

Copyright © 2010 by The Child's World®
All rights reserved. No part of this book may be reproduced or utilized in any form or by any means without written permission from the publisher.

Printed in the United States of America in Mankato, Minnesota.
November 2009
F11460

LIBRARY OF CONGRESS CATALOGING-IN-PUBLICATION DATA
Lindeen, Mary.
  Europe / by Mary Lindeen.
    p. cm. — (Earth's continents)
  Includes index.
  ISBN 978-1-60253-350-9 (library bound : alk. paper)
  1. Europe—Juvenile literature. I. Title.
  D1051.L53 2010
  940—dc22   2009030012